The Lessons Of Souls

A Journey Through Karma

Ashmit Kaur

Made with ❤ on the BookLeaf Publishing Platform
www.bookleafpub.in
www.bookleafpub.com

Dedication

*To those who walk the path of the soul with love,
wisdom, and grace.
May you find peace in every step of your journey.*

Preface

"In the stillness of the universe, we are all bound by the invisible threads of karma, shaping our lives with each thought, word, and action. This collection of poems, 'The Lessons of the Soul,' is a reflection of my own journey through life's most profound lessons—love, loss, joy, and sorrow. I also understood them by reading novels, stories, spiritual books and hearing to podcasts regarding spirituality, karma, past lives and many more. Through these verses, I explore how karma weaves the fabric of our existence, connecting us to each other, to the past, and to the future.

Each poem is a stepping - stone on the path of self-discovery, offering reflections on themes of soulmates, betrayal, sadness, faith, and the timeless nature of our emotions and relationships. These poems are not just an exploration of life's highs and lows but a reminder of the profound interconnectedness of all beings."

Acknowledgements

"I would like to express my deepest gratitude to my family for their unwavering love and support throughout this journey. To my mother, whose wisdom and encouragement inspired the very foundation of this book, thank you for always believing in me.
To my friends, who have shared in my moments of joy and sorrow, and to the teachers, past and present, who have guided me on my spiritual path—this book is as much yours as it is mine. Lastly, to the readers who embark on this journey of self-reflection and growth, I hope these poems offer you as much insight as they have offered me."

1. Karma

The Echo of Karma

In the quiet still of the cosmic play,
Every deed returns, no debt will stray.
A gentle touch, a word unkind,
The universe keeps them all in mind.

Beneath the stars, where secrets sleep,
The whispers of choices softly creep.
A flame of truth, a shadow of lies,
All find their path beneath the skies.

The hand that gives, the heart that mends,
Shapes the journey where the story bends.
For deeds are seeds, both dark and bright,
That bloom in time, in shadow or light.

So tread with grace, for paths entwine,
And the soul's own mirror will always shine.
In the quiet still of the cosmic play,
Karma watches, come what may.

The Threads of Karma

In the loom of time, threads intertwine,
Actions ripple, their echoes align.
A whisper turns to a roaring tide,
No truth nor lie can forever hide.

Beneath the sun, each shadow is cast,
What you sow today becomes your past.
Hands that harm, hearts that heal,
Life's ledger knows what we conceal.

The wheel turns slow, but justice wakes,
From seeds of kindness, the harvest takes.
Though unseen forces guide the flame,
Each deed returns, no soul untamed.

So, walk with care, let mercy bloom,
The fruits of love dispel the gloom.
For in this cycle, vast and grand,
Karma writes with an unseen hand.

2. Destiny

Beneath the stars, where silence hums,
Destiny waits, as the wheel turns.
Each choice a thread, each act a spark,
Drawing patterns in light and dark.

Karma's hands weave day by day,
Guiding steps along the way.
The wrongs we mend, the love we show,
Shape the roads where our souls will go.

Destiny speaks not in command,
But whispers soft through time's demand.
It bends to justice, yields to grace,
Revealing truths we cannot erase.

No path is locked, no fate is sealed,
For karma wields the greater shield.
From shadows deep to skies of fire,
Our deeds ignite what we desire.

The echoes linger, soft yet clear,
Of every smile, of every tear.
And as we walk, the story grows,
A tale of reaping what we chose.

So plant your seeds with care, with heart,
For destiny waits where journeys start.
Its shape is yours its soul is free—
Karma's gift to eternity.

3. Love

First love blooms, so pure, so bright,
Karma whispers, day and night.
In hearts unguarded, feelings grow,
A karmic tale, all set to flow.

The touch, the glance, the stolen kiss,
The kind of love that feels like bliss.
Yet within its beauty, hidden deep,
Are lessons that the heart must keep.

What we give, what we take,
In love's first dance, what's at stake?
For karma watches, as hearts entwine,
Guiding the love that's so divine.

Though first love may be fleeting, fast,
It leaves behind a shadow cast.
A lesson learned, a heart that grows,
Through joy and pain, through love that glows.

For in the end, the first love fades,
But karma's hand, it never sways.
The feelings linger, though the time has gone,
The soul moves forward, carrying on.

So, cherish the love that came and went,
For in it, karma's grace is spent.
First love, though brief, is never lost,
It returns again, at any cost.

Love is the echo of deeds we've done,
A bond that grows when hearts have won.
It blooms from kindness, fades from strife,
A karmic dance that shapes our life.

In every glance, in every touch,
The seeds we plant, they grow so much.
For love is earned, not freely given,
A reflection of the way we've lived and driven.

Each smile we share, each tear we've cried,
Leaves a trace, where hearts collide.
What we give returns in time,
For love's true power is born from rhyme.

So, sow with grace, with open heart,
For love's a mirror, a work of art.
And in its light, we come to see,
The karmic truth of what will be.

4. Death

Death is the end, yet not the close,
A shift in life, where balance grows.
A final step, yet not the last,
For what we sow, returns at last.

The soul's journey, long and wide,
Ends not in darkness, but on the other side.
Each breath we've taken, every choice we've made,
Shapes the peace where we'll be laid.

Through death, the karmic wheel does turn,
The lessons lived, the truths we learn.
What we've given, what we've taken,
In this moment, is awakened.

For death is but a bridge, not a fall,
A return to balance, to the universal call.
So in its arms, we find our rest,
A karmic cycle, at its best.

Death is the end, yet not the close,
A shift in life, where balance grows.
The soul that leaves, the body still,
Fulfills its fate, its karmic will.

What we've sown through every life,
Comes full circle, without strife.
No judgment harsh, no fate too grim,
Only the quiet of a soul's hymn.

The cycle turns, both slow and fast,
Each life, a lesson, meant to last.
In death, the karmic truth is clear—
We return to what we hold dear.

For in the end, we all must face,
The reckoning, the final grace.
A peace that comes from all we've done,
And in the end, we are all one.

5. Lessons in Life

Through every trial, through every fall,
Life whispers lessons to us all.
In moments dark, in light so bright,
We learn to walk, we learn to fight.

With every tear, a wisdom grows,
From all the pain, our strength bestows.
The broken paths, the hearts that mend,
Each step we take, we transcend.

The bitter winds that pierce the soul,
Reveal the way to make us whole.
In silent hours, in joy, in strife,
We find the truth that shapes our life.

So let each moment teach and guide,
In life's vast river, let us glide.
For in the end, we'll come to see,
The lessons learned, they set us free.

6. Soulmates

Two souls meet where fate has led,
Bound by the threads of lives once said.
In silent whispers, they reconnect,
A karmic bond that time can't deflect.

Through many lifetimes, hearts did roam,
Now reunited, they find their home.
Each glance a spark, each touch a flame,
A dance of souls, no one to blame.

The pain of past lives lingers near,
Yet in their union, all becomes clear.
For love's deep roots grow through the strife,
A karmic circle that shapes their life.

With every step, they heal and grow,
The lessons learned, the truths they know.
In each other, they find their place,
Soulmates bound by time and grace.

For Karma weaves its threads so fine,
Uniting hearts through every line.
So, when they meet, they'll understand,
Their love was written in time's hand.

7. Past Lives

In past lives, we lived and learned,
The lessons lived, the bridges burned.
What we sowed, what we gained,
Echoes now in the heart, unchained.

Each life a chapter, every choice a seed,
From past to present, we plant the need.
For karma's hand, both kind and harsh,
Guides us through each life's arch.

The wounds we carry, the love we seek,
Trace the paths where souls grow weak.
Yet in each step, the cycle's clear,
The past returns, its whispers near.

In every memory, a truth remains,
The ties we sever, the hearts we've trained.
Through countless lifetimes, we are reborn,
Until the lessons learned leave us worn.

So, tread with care, for fate will find,
The echoes of the past, intertwined.
In the mirror of time, we see the clue,
That past lives guide all we do.

8. Betrayal

A broken trust, a heart laid bare,
Karma waits with quiet care.
The lies once spoken, the pain once sown,
Return to haunt, a debt unknown.

The whispers linger, the scars remain,
What we give, we must regain.
For betrayal's sting, so sharp, so deep,
Wakes the soul from its silent sleep.

What we took, what we betrayed,
Returns in time, as debts are paid.
The heart that breaks, the soul that cries,
The karma found beneath the lies.

Yet in the darkness, lessons grow,
Through pain and loss, we come to know,
That betrayal, though it tears apart,
Is but a mirror to the heart.

So let the truth be held with care,
For Karma watches, always fair.
In the end, the broken will mend,
And betrayal's wound will find its end.

9. Sadness

Sadness lingers where hearts have wept,
Karma watches, where pain is kept.
The tears we shed, the sorrow we bear,
Are but echoes of the lives we wear.

In quiet moments, grief takes hold,
A karmic weight, both young and old.
What we've lost, what we've forsaken,
Returns in time, our hearts awaken.

Through every loss, through every ache,
The soul will bend but never break.
For in the dark, a light will shine,
A karmic gift, the path divine.

Sadness teaches, though it may sting,
That from the hurt, new growth will spring.
The pain we feel, the tears we cry,
Will one day fade, as time goes by.

For Karma holds the wounds we bear,
And in its balance, we'll repair.
Through every sorrow, we will find,
That sadness leaves, but peace will bind.

10. Anger

Anger burns with a fierce, bright flame,
Karma watches, it knows the game.
The fury that rises, the rage we hold,
Is a story of actions, both new and old.

What we lash out, what we release,
Creates a ripple, no inner peace.
The words we speak, the actions we take,
Leave a mark that time will make.

For anger, though it may feel right,
Returns in shadows, out of sight.
What we've cast into the storm,
Will circle back, in a different form.

Karma waits with steady grace,
A lesson learned, a calm embrace.
The fire we kindle will one day die,
And in its ashes, we'll wonder why.

So guard your heart, and still the mind,
For anger's course is cruel and blind.
In time, the storm will find its way,
And peace will come to those who pray.

11. Marriage

In vows we speak, in hearts we bind,
Karma weaves, the ties that bind.
Through love and trust, the promises grow,
But what we sow, we reap, we know.

Two souls unite, through joy and strife,
To learn the lessons of a shared life.
The past may linger, the future unclear,
Yet together, they face each fear.

What we give, what we take,
Shapes the bond we choose to make.
In marriage, love is both soft and strong,
A karmic dance, where we belong.

Through trials faced, through paths we tread,
Karma whispers what lies ahead.
The love we offer, the peace we seek,
Is mirrored in the hearts we keep.

So, cherish the vows, with truth and grace,
For marriage holds a sacred place.
In every moment, Karma's hand,
Guides the hearts that understand.

12. Depression

In shadows deep, the soul does hide,
Karma watches, where pain resides.
The weight we carry, the tears we keep,
Are echoes of wounds too deep to speak.

The past, unhealed, casts a long, dark veil,
A karmic shadow, a storm, a gale.
Each step we take, heavy and slow,
Is shaped by what we've yet to know.

In moments of silence, the heart cries loud,
A soul submerged, beneath a cloud.
The struggles we face, the battles within,
Are the echoes of where we've been.

Yet through the dark, a light will rise,
A karmic balance, a soul that tries.
For every wound, for every tear,
Healing comes, as peace draws near.

The cycle turns, slow but true,
Through every sorrow, we're made new.
For depression, though deep and strong,
Will fade in time, as we belong.

Karma's hand, though gentle and firm,
Leads the way, through each long term.
The past will heal, the heart will mend,
And in the end, peace will transcend.

13. Fight

In every fight, a truth is found,
Karma's hand, it spins around.
The battle fought, the anger raw,
Leaves behind a lasting flaw.

What we strike, what we defend,
Shapes the path, the means, the end.
In every clash, a lesson stirs,
Through fury's voice, the soul confers.

The words we throw, the actions taken,
Are seeds of conflict, once awakened.
For every war, whether won or lost,
Carries the price, the karmic cost.

Yet in the fight, we learn to see,
The part of us that longs to be free.
Each battle fought, each fight endured,
Brings wisdom earned, a soul secured.

The storm will pass, the winds will change,
What was once close will rearrange.
For Karma watches, with steady eye,
What we send out, returns, by and by.

So, fight with heart, but choose with care,
For in the end, it's love we share.
The karmic circle, ever wide,
Will guide us to the other side.

14. Relationship

In every bond, a truth is sewn,
Karma's threads, unseen, are grown.
The ties we form, the hearts we touch,
Shape the paths we love so much.

Each relationship, a karmic dance,
A meeting born of fate, not chance.
Through joy and sorrow, pain and peace,
The cycle of love will never cease.

What we give, what we take,
What we heal, what we break,
Each action stirs the heart's own song,
And in its rhythm, we belong.

In every friendship, in every fight,
Karma watches through day and night.
What we offer in trust or fear,
Returns to us, both far and near.

For love, though fragile, is pure and true,
The bonds we forge will see us through.
In the end, the circle finds its close,
A karmic peace, a love that grows.

So, cherish the ties, both soft and strong,
For relationships teach us where we belong.
Karma weaves through every thread,
Guiding the hearts that have been led.

15. Child

A child is born with eyes so wide,
Karma whispers, as hearts collide.
In innocence, the soul takes flight,
Carrying lessons from endless night.

The past they bring, though pure of heart,
Is shaped by what came from the start.
For every life, a karmic thread,
Guides each step, each word that's said.

The love we give, the care we show,
Sown the seeds of what will grow.
A child, though small, is bound by fate,
To learn and love, to learn and wait.

In every touch, in every smile,
The karma lingers, mile by mile.
What we offer, what we teach,
Is the foundation each soul will reach.

The child, so pure, yet wise beyond,
Carries the echoes of what's gone.
Through each new dawn, through every day,
Karma leads them on their way.

For the lessons passed, from heart to heart,
Are written in the soul's own chart.
So, nurture with love, with care and grace,
For in the child, all lives embrace.

16. Teacher

A teacher's words, both wise and true,
Karma's lessons, passed to you.
Through every lesson, through every word,
The soul is shaped, the heart is stirred.

The knowledge given, the paths we show,
Carry the seeds of what we know.
What we teach, what we learn,
Returns to us, in time to burn.

The wisdom shared, the truths we seek,
Echo through those who listen, meek.
For every lesson, every test,
Karma watches, guides the quest.

A teacher's hand, a guiding light,
Leads the way through dark and bright.
In every student, a spark remains,
The fire of knowledge, the loss, the gains.

So, teach with care, with heart, with soul,
For in each word, we make the whole.
The lessons passed, from hand to hand,
Shape the future, the mind, the land.

Karma's balance, firm and sure,
Ensures the wisdom will endure.
For the teacher, too, must learn and grow,
As the karmic cycle continues to flow.

17. Time

Time moves forward, yet stands still,
Karma watches, as we fulfill.
The clock that ticks, the hours that pass,
Are reflections of deeds in the glass.

Each moment lived, each choice we make,
Shapes the future, for karma's sake.
In the silence, the past calls loud,
While the present wears a shroud.

What we sow in fleeting time,
Is written in the stars, in rhyme.
Through every second, every breath,
We move closer to life and death.

Time is a river, forever flowing,
Karma's hand, ever knowing.
The seeds we plant, the love we give,
Shape the world, help us to live.

Though time may fly, and moments fade,
The lessons remain, firmly laid.
For karma turns the wheel so slow,
Guiding each soul where it must go.

So, cherish the time, both soft and fierce,
For through its passage, hearts will pierce.
Karma's gaze will never stray,
It watches time and shows the way.

18. Faith

Faith is the light that guides the way,
Karma waits, as night turns day.
Through trust we walk, through hope we soar,
A karmic path, forevermore.

In moments of doubt, in times of fear,
Faith whispers softly, "I am here."
The heart believes, though eyes may fail,
Karma watches, as we sail.

What we hold, what we believe,
Shapes the world we choose to weave.
Through faith, the impossible seems near,
Karma's hand is always clear.

In every prayer, in every sigh,
Faith rises, and never dies.
For the soul that trusts, the heart that knows,
Karma's grace forever grows.

Through faith, the road is long and wide,
Yet with each step, we're by its side.
For in the end, what we believe,
Karma brings, what we receive.

So trust the path, though it may bend,
For faith and karma both transcend.
In every step, in every fall,
Faith leads the way and conquers all.

19. Like

We are what we like, and in this truth,
Karma molds the heart of youth.
The things we cherish, the paths we choose,
Shape the life we gain or lose.

In every preference, in every sigh,
Karma whispers, and we reply.
What we adore, what we pursue,
Is a reflection of what's true.

Through likes and wants, the soul is led,
By passions and dreams, we're gently fed.
Yet karma watches, ever near,
To guide the heart and calm the fear.

For in our likes, a story's told,
A tale of desires, both young and old.
What we attract, we must return,
Through joy we love, through pain we learn.

So, choose with care, the things you seek,
For in them, your heart will speak.
What you like, what you adore,
Shapes the future, forevermore.

Karma listens, with patient grace,
To every like, to every trace.
And in the end, it will reveal,
What we've chosen, what we feel.

20. Write

In ink and words, the past is told,
Each page a story, both new and old.
With every stroke, a truth unfolds,
A karmic thread, a tale of old.

What we write reflects the soul,
A mirror of the heart's own goal.
Each sentence formed, each word we choose,
Shows what we give, what we lose.

The ink flows deep, like time's own tide,
Each mark a step we cannot hide.
What we create, what we compose,
The seeds we plant, the path it shows.

Through writing's power, our deeds are sown,
In the pages, all we've known.
For every word has weight and care,
Each thought we shape hangs in the air.

So, write with wisdom, write with grace,
For Karma watches, it leaves no trace.
The stories we tell will one day return,
In the written words, our souls discern.

21. Mother

A mother's love, so pure, so vast,
Karma watches, through ages past.
Her hands that hold, her heart that heals,
Shape the soul, as fate reveals.

Through sleepless nights and endless care,
Her spirit weaves a love so rare.
For every child, a karmic thread,
Tied to the words the mother said.

What she gives, what she shows,
Is carried with the child, it grows.
Her love, her pain, her sacrifice,
Returns to her, in karmic spice.

The lessons taught, the strength she shares,
Echo through time, through prayers and cares.
For in a mother's love, so deep,
Are secrets of the soul we keep.

Though her path may twist and turn,
Her love's the flame that will always burn.
Karma sees what the mother gives,
And in return, the soul shall live.

For every act, both large and small,
A mother's love is felt by all.
Karma's grace, so kind and true,
Guides the mother's heart, anew.